Walt Disney's Comics and Stories
No. 666, March 2006
Published monthly by Gemstone Publishing,
© 2006 Disney Enterprises, Inc., except where noted.

ISBN 1-888472-19-7

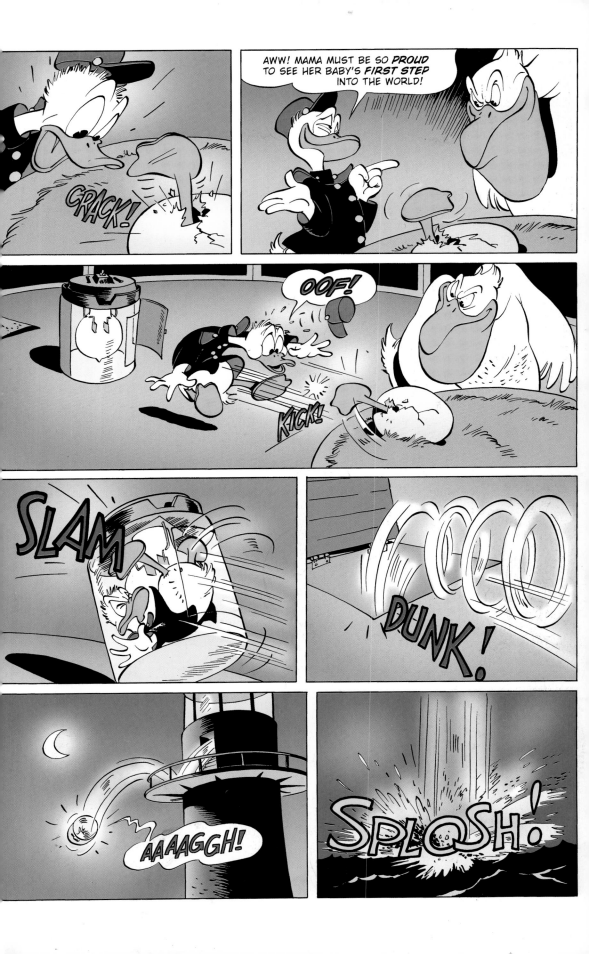

GEMSTONE PUBLISHING

presents

YOUR FAVORITE DISNEY COMICS

© 2006 Disney
Enterprises Inc.

Delivered right to your door!

We know how much you enjoy visiting your local comic shop, but wouldn't it be nice to have your favorite Disney comics delivered to you? Subscribe today and we'll send the latest issues of your favorite comics directly to your doorstep. And if you would still prefer to browse through the latest in comic art but aren't sure where to go, check out the Comic Shop Locator Service at www.diamondcomics.com/csls or call 1-888-COMIC-BOOK.

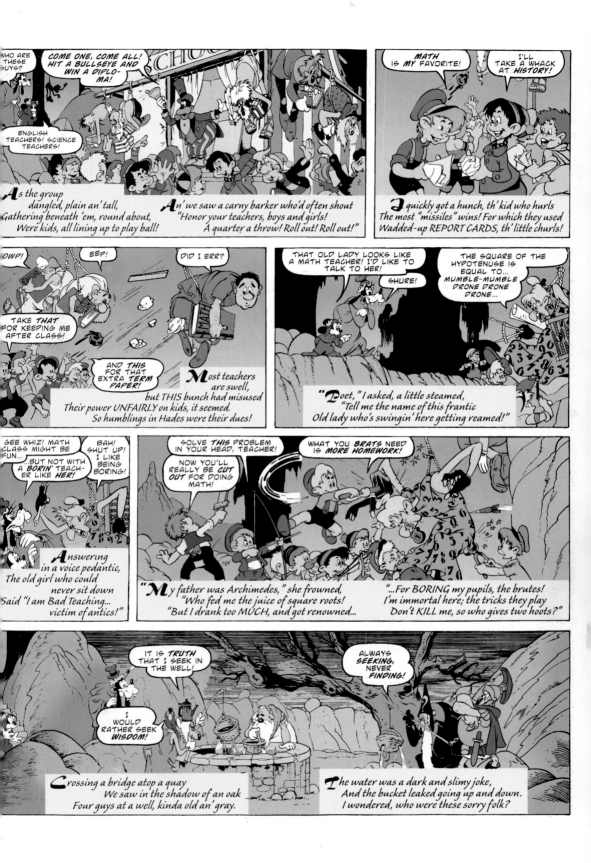

As the group
   dangled, plain an' tall,
Gathering beneath 'em, round about,
   Were kids, all lining up to play ball!

An' we saw a carny barker who'd often shout
   "Honor your teachers, boys and girls!
      A quarter a throw! Roll out! Roll out!"

I quickly got a hunch, th' kid who hurls
   The most "missiles" wins! For which they used
      Wadded-up REPORT CARDS, th' little churls!

Most teachers
   are swell,
but THIS bunch had misused
   Their power UNFAIRLY on kids, it seemed.
      So humblings in Hades were their dues!

"Poet," I asked, a little steamed,
   "Tell me the name of this frantic
      Old lady who's swingin' here getting reamed!"

Answering
   in a voice pedantic,
The old girl who could
   never sit down
Said "I am Bad Teaching...
      victim of antics!"

"My father was Archimedes," she frowned,
   "Who fed me the juice of square roots!
      "But I drank too MUCH, and got renowned...

"...For BORING my pupils, the brutes!
   I'm immortal here; the tricks they play
      Don't KILL me, so who gives two hoots?"

Crossing a bridge atop a quay
      We saw in the shadow of an oak
   Four guys at a well, kinda old an' gray.

The water was a dark and slimy joke,
      And the bucket leaked going up and down.
   I wondered, who were these sorry folk?

*This hound of the mists could bark an' bay
From three big mouths! While down below,
A crowd of souls in the deep mud lay!*

*They'd have loved to scram, but could they? No!
The big dog chomped each one who tried!
And did they howl? Like dentists' patients! Whoa!*

*The Circle of Gluttons lay alongside.
Full o' folks who, in life, had loved their sweets!
Their penance came in bein' plied*

*With more food than even they could eat!
Cakes and pizzas by the score...
Rivers with milk an' honey replete!*

YOU'RE GONNA EAT, LIKE IT OR NOT!

*Lots of guys could
chow down no more—
Havin' had their fill
of taste temptation!
But darn the luck, a demon bore*

*Down on them
in wicked animation!
With a turkey baster, he pumped folks up
Full of gravy... enough to drown a nation!*

TA-RA! TA-RA!

*As we left them all to their dismal sup,
Our ears were hit by a noisy blast!
First a trumpet call, then a loud gallop!*

RUN FOR IT!

*'Twas the hounds of Hades! As I cast
My eyes ahead, I saw the mutts
In packs of thousands, dashing past!*

MOVE, GOOFY! **HE WON'T LET ME!**

*Their duty it was to bite the butts
Of the guys who were enslaved down here!
Cerberus, barking like he was nuts,*

*Chomped poor Goofy in the rear!
"Feet, do yer stuff!" he yelled aloud.
"This doggie's foes have lots ta fear!"*

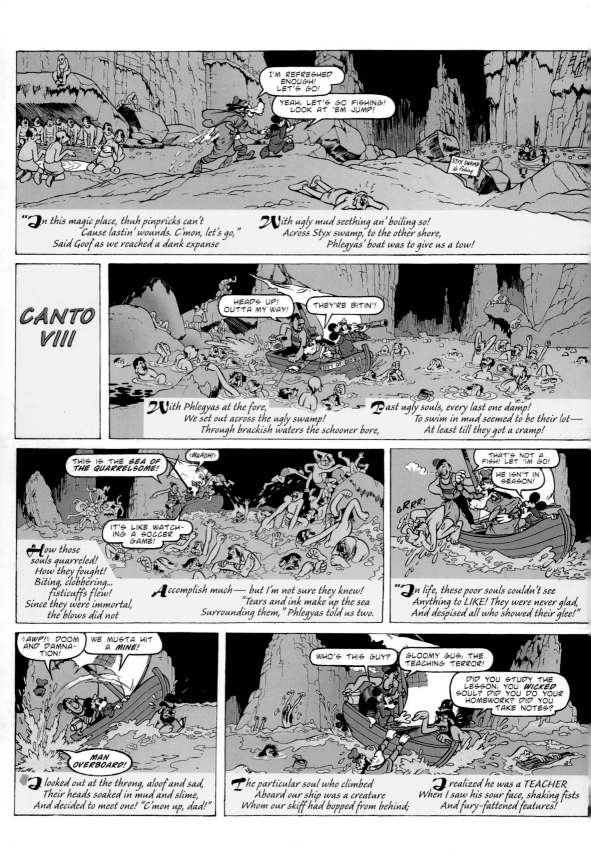

"In this magic place, thuh pinpricks can't
  Cause lastin' wounds. C'mon, let's go,"
Said Goof as we reached a dank expanse

With ugly mud seething an' boiling so!
  Across Styx swamp, to the other shore,
    Phlegyas' boat was to give us a tow!

CANTO VIII

With Phlegyas at the fore,
  We set out across the ugly swamp!
    Through brackish waters the schooner bore,

Past ugly souls, every last one damp!
  To swim in mud seemed to be their lot—
    At least till they got a cramp!

How those
souls quarreled!
  How they fought!
Biting, clobbering...
    fisticuffs flew!
Since they were immortal,
  the blows did not

Accomplish much — but I'm not sure they knew!
  "Tears and ink make up the sea
    Surrounding them," Phlegyas told us two.

"In life, these poor souls couldn't see
  Anything to LIKE! They were never glad,
    And despised all who showed their glee!"

I looked out at the throng, aloof and sad,
  Their heads soaked in mud and slime,
    And decided to meet one! "C'mon up, dad!"

The particular soul who climbed
  Aboard our ship was a creature
    Whom our skiff had bopped from behind;

I realized he was a TEACHER
  When I saw his sour face, shaking fists
    And fury-fattened features!

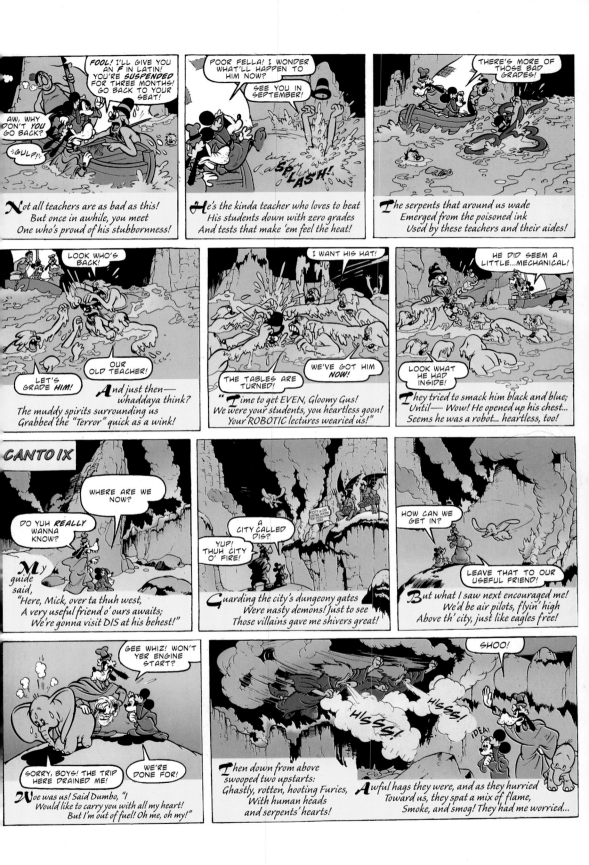

...Till a great IDEA to me came!
I tied the Furies fast to Dumbo's sides;
Using them to help us was my aim!

*L*ike jet engines, they gave us rides
By spitting their mighty breath out behind!
(See th' allegory that in here hides?)

CANTO X

*A*s we flew, we looked below to find
Spirits in cradle-like tombs, aglow
With eternal flames! "Say, I wouldn't mind...

...the BURNS so much," I whispered low;
"If I were IMMORTAL, they wouldn't LAST!"
"Yer right, Mick," Goofy said, "but know—

THIS IS THUH PUNISHMENT FER FOLKS WITH *FIERY* TEMPERS!

...thuh HEAT still hurts,
an' THAT'S never past!
These ghosts were all HOTHEADS in life;
Now they're PUNISHED with heat!
I'D be downcast!"

LOOK! ANOTHER LOST SOUL!

GAWRSH! HE LOOKS... *HAPPY!*

*W*hat we saw next distracted us from strife!
Through Hades' flaming kingdom drove
A fella LAUGHING— sarcastic-like!

WHAT'S SO FUNNY, MISTER?

HOT-CHA-CHA! READ THE VERSES AND FIND OUT!

*"W*ithout fear," I said,
"through FLAMES you rove!"
"Is this really a FUN place to park it?"
"I'm a match," he said, "Manufactured by those...

...with a MONOPOLY on the match market!
They've got NO competition! Strike my head
And you'll find you can never spark it!"

I WANNA TRY IT!

FORGET IT! I WON'T LIGHT!

"I'm INCOMBUSTIBLE!
My masters' bread
Keeps coming whether or not I work!
I'm FIREPROOF... and well-read!"

"*What gives you*
        the RIGHT," we heard him pout,
"*To pass ALIVE through this infernal clime*
While I'M a ghost? >Hmph!< Sort that out!"

"*Don,*" I said,
        "*It's a sorta DREAM-TIME*
That brought me here; I'm MORTAL because
I'm REAL—and the DREAM is MINE!"

"*You're just*
        a dream-image: unreal and flawed!
Back you go, Duck!" WRONG thing to say;
        He didn't LIKE our layin' down the law!

We shut him in;
        he thrashed and brayed,
Showing his penance-worthy temper!
He roared like a moped; our ears he frayed!

We hoped to escape someplace better!
        But as we hustled to safety fast,
A grumbling ghost duck followed after!

In our haste to flee, we overpassed
        The boundary, SKIPPING a canto before
We knew it! Reaching a stream at last,

We met the grim, proud Minotaur;
        Though in my dream, the big bull-man
Was a "SITTING Bull": Hiawatha's pa!

We reached Canto Twelve,
        and as we scanned
The air, three happy chappies were seen;
On a flying serape, the sky they spanned!

The first man was Panchito, keen
        And eager, sombrero on his head—
Firing his pistols around the scene!

He greeted me with arms outspread,
And a sincere "Caramba!" in Spanish!
"Arriba, caballero, back atcha," I said!

José gave me a handshake clannish:
"To see you, Senhor, is the best!"
(In Brazil, senhor means "Mister," I managed.)

We reached out over the hot spring horrid;
A river that blazed with the color of blood,
And pulled Don up from destiny torrid!

No sooner had he escaped the flood
Than he said: "Mouse, you can't duck ME!
I found my way back to you, bud!"

Oops! Just then, our third flying guest
Clumsily put the wrong foot forward!
He began to slip down toward a deep abyss!

"Now I get my vengeance, see?
You say I'm a FIGMENT
of your IMAGINATION!
I don't care what kinda dream this be—

I think I'm REAL! My expectation
Is that we'll SWAP PLACES; YOU stay here
While D. Duck returns to
our mortal nation!"

Said I,
"It's not that easy, I fear!"
"I must do a good deed before I can leave!
YOU don't know GOOD from a kick in the rear!"

The serape flew! As off it weaved,
I pondered Don's fate. Dream-image he was;
Yet his final fate felt like a TEST for me!

"Can we save him, Goofy?" I asked at once.
"Perhaps," said Goof, "but fergit that now!
Thuh FOREST ahead's a-CALLIN' us!"

Along the lonely plain we plowed
Until we came across a wood
That reminded us of parks we found

Back home in Mouseton! Bits of food
And gum wrappers lay amid the grass;
Barkless trees lent a scary mood.

*The flock around him fell to battle;
Showing the temper that brought Don here,
They pecked Goofy till he rattled!*

*Master Goof, unable to clear
The air, soon lost his firm resolve.
He fainted, wrecked by wear and tear!*

*At last the cursed flock dissolved;
To scare them, from a nearby tree
I broke a branch— but it evolved!*

*The tree limb spoke! "You're hurting me!
You think your scarin' plan's a pippin—
But I don't like it! Hully gee!..."*

*"Bruise me, an' you'll get a whippin'!"
Humbled, I said, "I never meant
"To hurt anyone with my grippin'!"*

*"Tell me, Bertie; what ill intent
Coulda turned you into a STICK
And left you a woodland malcontent?"*

*"As a mortal,"
said Bertie, "I loved playin' tricks,
And this is how jokers pay penance here:
Turned into parts of trees, Unca Mick!"*

*"But the NEXT step is what we really fear;
Cut down by lumberjacks, sanded and sawed!
It doesn't do much for good cheer!"*

*"We're split apart into multiple boards,
Then nailed back together as one!
It's almost enough to make me sore!"*

WOW! THE *BLUE FAIRY!* DID YOU COME TO SAVE THESE PRANKSTERS?

YES, Mickey! They have REPENTED—a truly good deed! So I will free them from their prison of wood!

The Wishing-Star Fairy!
How she shone!
With one graceful, magical gesture,
The wooden scraps that had lain prone

On the floor hopped up with pleasure!
Little boys out from within them stood;
Regaining the form they treasured!

HOORAY!

WE'RE FREE!

WE AREN'T *DESKS* ANYMORE!

÷URK!

Do no harm to the children!

STOP! DIDN'T YA HEAR?

As Bertie finished his tale so blue,
There came a miraculous sight
Amid that raucous and rioting crew!

From the sky, a star so bright
Descended, speaking in gentle tones
And stunning us with angelic light!

"*Any child who is not good,*"
Said the Fairy, warm and true,
"*Might just as well be made*
of wood!"

"*Now leave this realm*
behind you
As long as you swear
to study hard
And of foolish wrongdoing
mind you!"

That goes for you too, Donald! Learn to keep your temper...

AND I CAN RETURN TO EARTH? OH, BROTHER!

"*Be even-tempered, son; discard*
Your side that would disdain poor Mick,"
The fairy charmed our rogue canard.

*Honest John, the fox so slick,
Watched the kids' redemption
And sought to play a no-good trick!*

*The fox showed his intentions
As he said, "Oh—studying's QUITE all right...
If you're DIM, or if you like TENSION!"*

*"The surest sign that one is BRIGHT
Is that one enjoys his PLAY!
So slack off and be idle, mites!"*

*I spoke up! "Kids, you'll rue th' day
You let that fox LURE ya with the bait
Of PHONY fun! I say— ix-nay!"*

*"Only one thing
can save ya from the fate
Of penance in Hades once again:
This cricket's warnings, wise an' great!"*

*The fox slunk off! For he knew when
Defeat was nigh! As for the lads,
Their virtue carried them home again!*

*"We gotta depart this scene so glad,"
Said Goofy, "an' continue our trip
Ta circles o' Hades a bit more SAD!"*

Outta the gloomy woods we slipped
  And reached a plain where scorching snow
    Down from the heavens zipped.

It seemed impossible onward to go,
  Until a kind sales fellow
    On us some caravan gear bestowed!

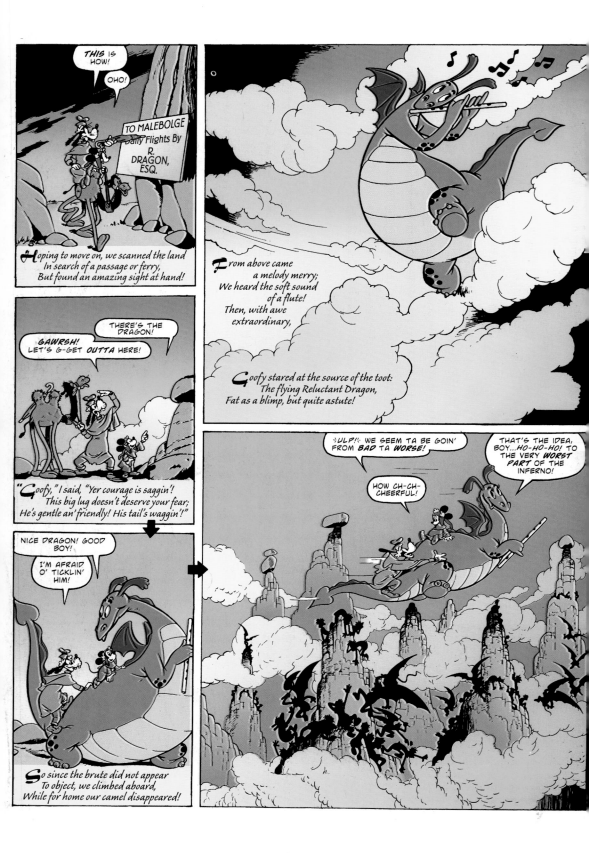

*U*p ahead, some fellas poked

FOOTBALL SCORES

MOUSETON - DUCKBURG	13	0	1
GOOSETOWN - GANDER FLATS	2	4	X
ST. CANARD - SWANSDOWN	6	1	1
EAST MALLARD - DRAKEVILLE	5	0	X
PORT HERON - GROUSE HILL	5	0	X

Around a signboard; with a burlap
Sack on the head of every bloke!

WELCOME TO THE PCIRCLE OF PFORTUNE PTELLERS!

WHAT THE DEVIL ARE THESE DEVILS DOING?

"*A*s you psee," Eega Beeva yukked,
"Here are punished with pcovered eyes
Pgamblers, false prophets and similar pclucks!"

*T*hen there came,
  with fiendish cries,
Some bat-winged demons
  out for fun!
They whirled the seers
  in circles wide

☆HAW!☆ YOU **SAID** YOU COULD SEE THE **FUTURE**, BUT NOW YOU CAN'T SEE A **THING!**

*A*nd cried,
"On earth, you fibbers SPUN
Tall tales to fool
  your many marks!
Now WE'LL spin YOU!
  Come, everyone!"

At last we made our escape from there!
Up an infernal hill we hiked
To reach an old tree, where

We met a little pig who liked
To play what he called violin jüve,
While his brother beside him fifed!

We watched Practical Pig arrive!
With Li'l Wolf, the brain-boy breathless
Warned of danger to their lives!

We heard a wolf-howl feckless—
The fearful foursome cowered,
Then dashed off, bold and reckless!

It was getting near the hour
When magpies roost on houses' eaves
And families dinner devour!

Big bad Zeke Wolf, king of thieves,
Fueled by eternal hunger, tried
A juicy pig meal to achieve!

"I'd say that's Hades' punishment
 For stealing what's not yours," I guessed.
As if to back up that intent,

A flock of stolen hens egressed
 From Big Bad's sack, and got to work
Delivering GNAWING regrets!

He hollered: "Bah! I've been a JERK!
 The birds I swiped are gettin' even!
My pig chase ended with no pork,

An' now I'm fit fer HALLOWEENIN'—
 Lookin' like a skeleton man!
I'm DONE with stealin'! I've seen REASON..."

"I'll be PEACEFUL as a lamb!"
 But— omigosh! A passing poacher
Vowed to give this "bird" the BLAM!

And so debate was brought to cloture!
 Now I saw that all these ills
Were meant to REFORM the old pig-roaster!

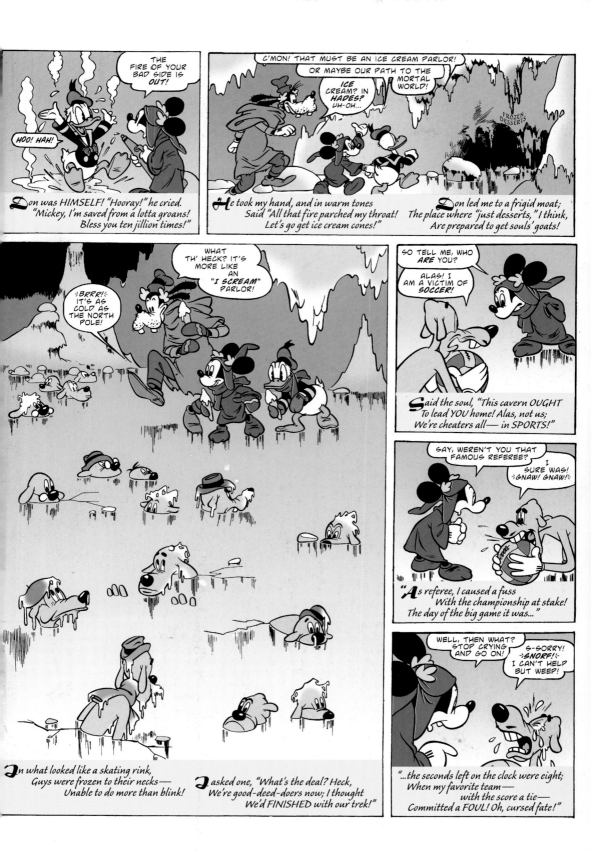

THE FIRE OF YOUR BAD SIDE IS OUT!

HOO! HAH!

Don was HIMSELF! "Hooray!" he cried.
"Mickey, I'm saved from a lotta groans!
Bless you ten jillion times!"

C'MON! THAT MUST BE AN ICE CREAM PARLOR!

OR MAYBE OUR PATH TO THE MORTAL WORLD!

ICE CREAM? IN HADES... UH-OH...

FROZEN DESSERTS

He took my hand, and in warm tones
Said "All that fire parched my throat!
Let's go get ice cream cones!"

Don led me to a frigid moat;
The place where "just desserts," I think,
Are prepared to get souls' goats!

WHAT TH' HECK? IT'S MORE LIKE AN "I SCREAM" PARLOR!

BRRR! IT'S AS COLD AS THE NORTH POLE!

In what looked like a skating rink,
Guys were frozen to their necks—
Unable to do more than blink!

I asked one, "What's the deal? Heck,
We're good-deed-doers now; I thought
We'd FINISHED with our trek!"

SO TELL ME, WHO ARE YOU?

ALAS! I AM A VICTIM OF SOCCER!

Said the soul, "This cavern OUGHT
To lead YOU home! Alas, not us;
We're cheaters all— in SPORTS!"

SAY, WEREN'T YOU THAT FAMOUS REFEREE?

I SURE WAS! GNAW! GNAW!

"As referee, I caused a fuss
With the championship at stake!
The day of the big game it was..."

WELL, THEN WHAT? STOP CRYING AND GO ON!

S-SORRY! SNORF! I CAN'T HELP BUT WEEP!

"...the seconds left on the clock were eight;
When my favorite team—
with the score a tie—
Committed a FOUL! Oh, cursed fate!"

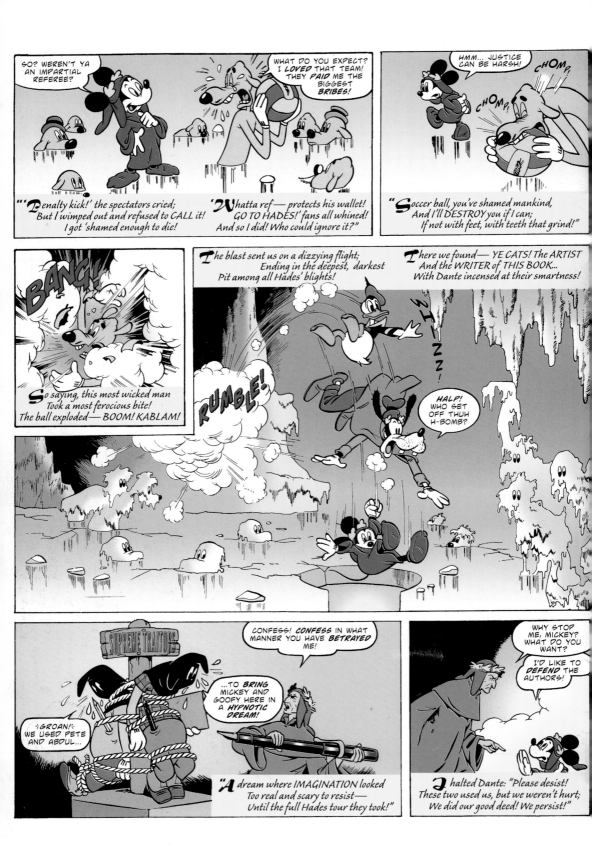

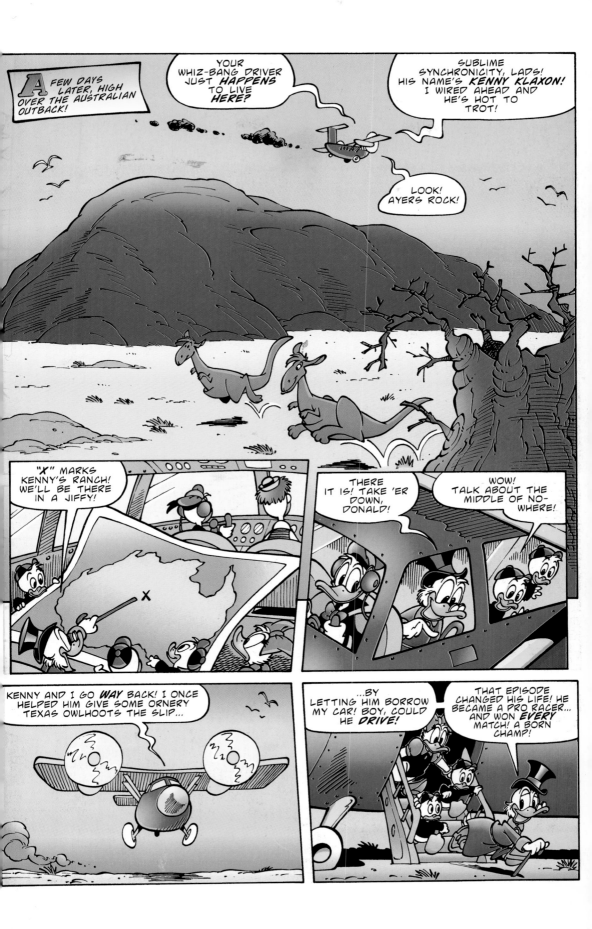

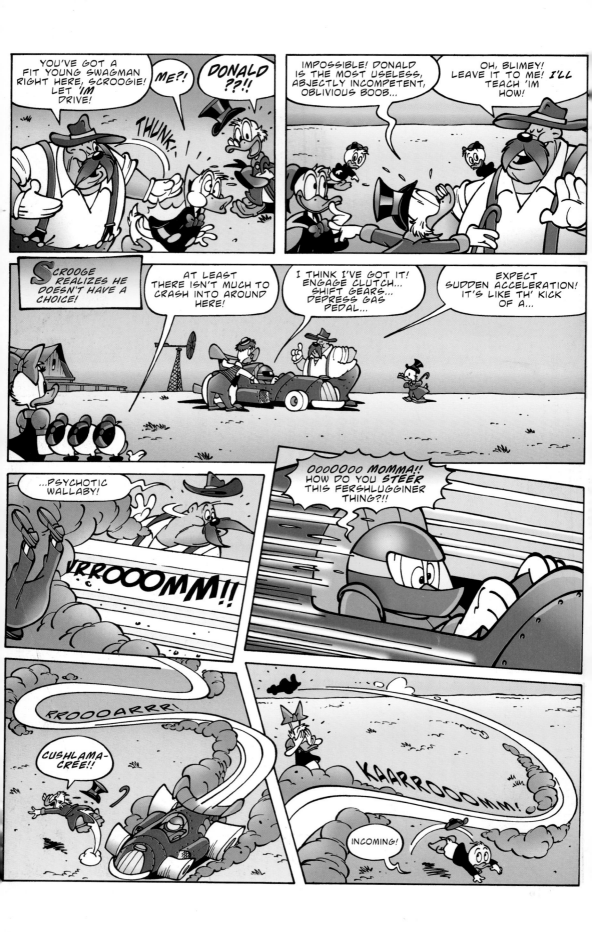

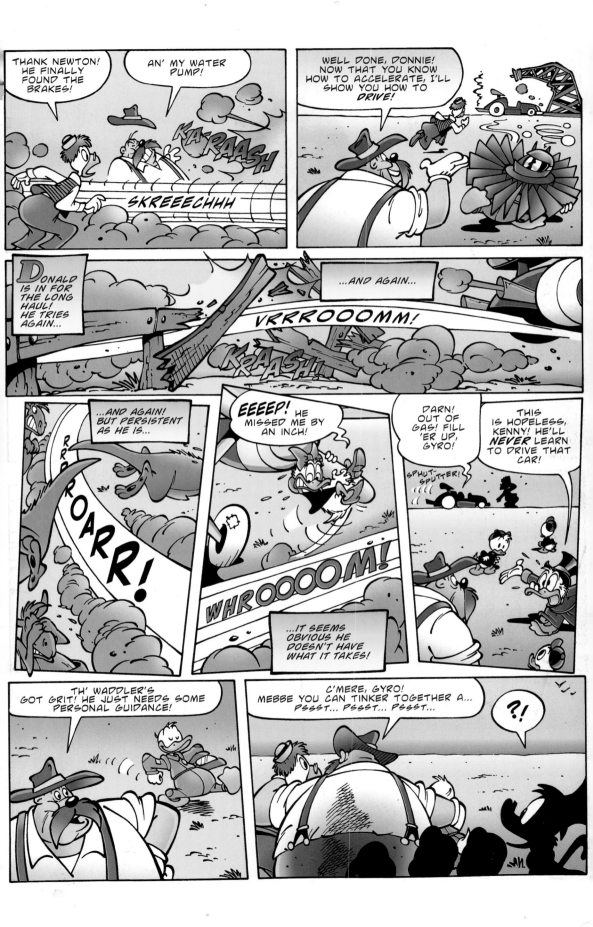